"These beautiful poems will lighten your soul and make your heart smile."
   —*Marci Shimoff, #1 NY Times bestselling author,* **Chicken Soup for the Woman's Soul.**

"I want to read aloud every poem in this book to everyone in the whole world. I know truth when I see it. Tony's poetry has reawakened in me a deeper sense of God's world. I am left only with myself and the mystery of how the simple can be so profound."
   —*Gloria Wendroff,* **Heavenletters.org**

"The beguiling subtitle *"twenty-seven poems by tony ellis and a couple by his dad"* give us a glimpse of the warm feeling and light-hearted spirit of this collection of poems by father and son. Tony's poems coax the reader into silent, soft depths of knowingness, which will at times, suspend your breath. He observes "the sacred" in what is simple and close by—a cat, a garden, or a bed-pillow. His father, Bob, finds silent rhythms and rippling lullabies in his beloved Welsh mountains and Yorkshire moors. If you love poetry, let this work guide you to find your own voice."
   —*Rodney Charles, author of the bestselling* **Every Day a Miracle Happens.**

"These poems were crafted by a deeply spiritual soul. They are populated by angels, gods, goddesses, "deep carpets of bluebells and wild onions," "infinity covered in a stranger's mask." Reading this book you will step into a world where "there are no bones in my hands, only light."

—*Diane Frank, award winning poet and author of* **Blackberries in the Dream House** *and* **The Winter Life of Shooting Stars.**

"Ellis' poems, like jewels—spare, serene and pristine in their beauty—need no particular setting. They reflect, like clear mirrors unhampered by distortion, the unity and connectedness of all things. Focusing on personal meditative experiences and daily activities, the poems in this collection playfully and longingly touch the edges of eternity. With a minimum of adornment and elaboration, the images presented in these poems move us as through a prism into the center of things. The speaker in these poems seeks the *oneness* and is nourished by his affinity to it."

—*Barbara Paul-Emile, Ph.D. Goldman Professor of English, Bentley College, MA, and author of* **Seer.**

there is
wisdom in walnuts

twenty-seven poems by tony ellis
and a couple by his dad

1st WORLD
LIBRARY
Literary Society

AUSTIN • FAIRFIELD • DELHI

there is wisdom in walnuts
copyright © 2004 tony ellis
except *the turning point* and *the lullaby of running water*
copyright © 2004 bob ellis

1st World Library
PO Box 2211
Fairfield, IA 52556
www.1stworldlibrary.com

Cover design and photography by Michael Yankaus
Graphics and layout by Tony Ellis

wisdom in walnuts website:
www.tonyellis.com

FIRST EDITION

Library of Congress Catalogue Card Number:
2003099440
ISBN: 1-59540-998-X

to my father, the poet
and to Maharishi, my teacher

table of contents

introduction

I cannot say much about the process of writing poetry except to say that it is as if I step through a gateway inside and into a place of certainty and revelation, thrill and expansion, where nothing and everything happen simultaneously. From there the poems seem to write themselves as if gifts from a greater, more creative self. My father also describes a similar experience when he writes about his favorite landscapes. That place exists inside all of us; it just needs waking up.

Other than that, I have to let the poems speak for themselves.

I hope they find a place to resonate inside of you.

tony ellis

dreaming...

A BEGINNING

I dreamed
I was dreaming
and then I awoke
and I was still
dreaming...

rivers can
show you
to flow
without
motion...

THERE IS WISDOM IN WALNUTS

there is wisdom in walnuts,
　brilliance in atoms

　　rivers can show you
　to flow
without motion

grass can be gentle
　and petals passionate

　　a million galaxies
　　　meet on the head of a pin

　and the space that's outside
is the same space within

there is
   no anger
      here,
         only love...

A PLACE OF PEACE

there is a place of peace
    inside of you
stretched thin and glorious
    like a straight line

when softly touched
    it explodes with radiance
and the warm glow of surety.

there is no fear
in this place of peace,
    only safety

there is no hope here,
    only certainty

there is no anger here,
    only love

• • •

in this place of peace
the promises of politicians
seem distant echoes,
    like tin cans
    blown along an empty alley

the smell of money turns
to a wafted scent of compassion,
and greed is distant
    like a burned out taillight

in this place of peace
you are warm and unafraid,
clear and courageous,
    happy and outrageous

all things are possible
    in this place of peace,
all energy inexhaustible,

• • •

and any insecurity
    blooms into magnificence

in this place of peace,
        you are me
        and we are everyone,
and the only certain thing
        is that *I am*,
        and always will be,
the source, course,
mother, son,
daughter and grandparent
of this my only child
        —the world

a
  brief flash
    of feather...
    and then
      she was gone...

HAWKS WATCHED ME

hawks watched me
    all the way to Denver

from fence posts and traffic signs,
they feigned indifference,
but the alertness in their eyes
betrayed their doing
of whatever task
the angels had given them

when I returned home,
I saw a brief flash of feather
in the pine tree
outside my window,
    and then she was gone

19

trip
    and fall
        into space,
            like a leaf
                hovering
                    from a tree...

SNEAKING FREE

perhaps
    I can sneak
unobserved
    into the light
and become accidentally aware

slip around a thought
and become somehow
    undefined

lie flat and undiscovered
while a cloud of recognition
    rolls over me

trip
  and fall into space,
  like a leaf
hovering from a tree
    —free

a
  thousand
  moons
  sigh
   in
    satisfaction...

A LOTUS PETAL OF LOVE

a seeming distant roar
    settles
        into silence

a thousand moons
    sigh
        in satisfaction

as the mother
    of my being
        moves

and a lotus petal of love
    floats
        pinkly
            through
                the fabric
        of my heart
        and lands
        gently
        on my mind

deep carpets
of bluebells
and wild onions...

CHILDHOOD MEMORY

I grew up in a world
 rubbed black by carbon,
with acrid air
and soot-stained streets

I breathed in smog,
tasted acid in rain,
saw green hills
stripped naked and bare

white sheep wore coats of grime

people coughed, and pale-faced,
 died young of old age

• • •

I played in mighty rivers
imagined from polluted streams,
stormed electric pylon castles,
reveled among broken glass
and stinking steel;
pram wheels were my chariots
and sticks my swords

and,
    secret in the woods
    on round hill,
    were deep carpets
    of bluebells
    and wild onions

I ONCE MET A GOD

have you ever stood
    naked as the dawn
but huge as cosmic space
with all the universe
    within you?

have you ever looked in a mirror
    and seen infinity
cloaked in a stranger's mask?

I once met a god
in the woods of Holland

he appeared before me
radiant and bejewelled
    like Krishna
with a shining gold crown
and a kind smile

I thought of all the Indian paintings
I had seen

        . . .

he was inside
and outside me
    at the same time
and his form was both solid
    and clear

his appearance was brief
    and his blessing short
but I have never forgotten him
    though it was many years
    before
    I revealed his secret

he hovers in my thoughts
as a gentle presence,
inexplicable and unimaginable,
    but real as flesh

IN MEDITATION

in
meditation
I don't exist

just stretched light
and a warm glow

a floating smile
in space
and a faint
sensation
on my
lips

my
    palms
        cup silence
           soft
               and thick...

THERE ARE NO BONES IN MY HAND

there are no bones
in my hands
        only light

my palms cup silence
    soft
            and
                    thick

I touch the earth
as only a memory
        of flesh

and my heart plays tag
        with the stars

warm

dark

and

silent...

MY CAMBODIAN GOD

I have a cambodian god
in my bedroom

I found him at T J Maxx,
black and alone
on a shelf
in the household aisle;
miserable,
between bright jugs
and blue bowls

for $9.50, plus tax,
I set him free,
adorned him with rudraksh beads,
tilacked him with sandalpaste,
washed him clean

now he sits,
warm dark and silent,
and watches over me while I sleep—
head and shoulders of an ancient culture
inexplicably at rest
in a Fairfield farmhouse

birds sing
in my orchard...

an apricot fills my mind

my thoughts are its warm, golden flesh
and my skin is smooth
and soft

birds sing in my orchard
with crisp green apple sounds

the sun shines
dappled on my boughs,
and my tongue tastes
the song
of the lonely cuckoo

the tips
   of my tears
      were sharp
         with joy...

AN ANGEL LAY UPON ME

an angel lay upon me
    as I slept

her weight was heavy
on my legs
and my body
was held down,
    while my spirit
    roamed free

an angel lay upon me
    as I cried

her weight
was in the fullness of the drops,
    but the tips of my tears
    were sharp with joy

. . .

an angel lay upon me
   as I died

her touch was soft
   as dew,
and my soul floated
   high and free
   as the angel
   that is me

A NEW WORLD

my hands
hold infinity
in a delicate touch
as if a new world
has been born there
and needs careful
handling
like a child

the air
    around
        breathed
            birdsong...

AFTER THE RAIN

I walked
on purple flowers
past leaves
shined green
by rain
the air around
breathed birdsong
and
as each call
shrank to silence
secret doors
to infinity
were opened
in my mind

fly
    towards
      that
        single
          star...

VENETIAN BLINDS

I lay at night
    and watch
a single star
    through venetian blinds

plastic cell bars
    guard me
    from cosmic dimension

I turn on the light

the world becomes inches
    defined by its thin glow

my mind,
    once reaching for the stars,
    shrinks and soaks
    into the absorbent rag of life

• • •

it is time to get up—
    I am a small child's toy
    that is wound and moves

tonight I vow to become fluid
    like transparent glue,
    and squeeze
    between sharp plastic bars—
    a stretched rubber soul;
evaporate into darkness
    and fly
towards that single star
    until its brightness
    burns me into infinite light
    and I fill the space
    between the stars
    like a thin
    vibrating membrane

A SINGLE DROP OF DEW

the light we see
reflected
in a single drop
of dew
is the pathway
to a million civilizations
whose voice
we never hear
except
in the gentle breath
of breeze
and the quiet hum
of life
infinitely growing

the
  silent
   sound
    of infinite
     life...

I CAN SEE THROUGH MY EYELIDS

.

I can see through my eyelids
    into distant worlds

spaceships of light
    float
across velvet blackness
    that hums
with the silent sound
    of infinite life

then the cat comes
    sneaking and squeaking
into my room
    and the dream returns

when I was a child
I lived a million lives
    seen through the darkness
    of my eyes pressed against the pillow

they stayed in my head
    as I ate breakfast
    and went to school

the war
in men's minds
stirred
the ghouls
of decay...

SATURDAY MARCH 15th—
ON THE EVE OF WAR

in the morning,
     as I sat in silence,
a dead man came beside me,
his form cold and gray,
     and I wondered
if the angel of death
had come for my soul

weird spirits
roamed the edge of my vision,
     gasping sobs of exhaled air,
as the war in men's minds
stirred the ghouls of decay

in the evening,
a rabbit threw its life
at the wheels of my car
     and was gone
in a quick bump of tire;
and a young boy named Jeffrey
died a pointless death,
     naked and alone,
in the cold morning air

a
   gentle
      kiss
         lays
            you
               blissfully
                  at the feet
                     of God...

THE PILLOWED PATH

there is
a pillowed path
to quietness
that floats
on the softness
of sound
and
with
a gentle kiss
lays you
blissfully
at the feet
of God

a
   child
      who
sneaked
into
   God's
      garden...

IN THE FACE OF GOD

I sit down to meditate,
     close my eyes,
and my soul is sucked
through a burning hole of light
     between my brows
and into the hugeness of space

a quick memory of the room
     where I sit
flits across my mind
then falls
     to the
     Earth
     below

the edges of my being
     are now defined
by a transparent line
     sketched thinly
     against the vastness,
which is somehow dark
     and full of light
     at the same time   . . .

I swell and vibrate
    with an energy
    that can only be love
my form
    is flexible
    and stretches out

I am standing
in the face of God—
    a force so terrifyingly large
    that I fear I will burst
    and be annihilated

unseen internal hands
    grasp the skin
    of my being
and hold on
    tight, afraid

I deflate and shrink
    back into ordinariness—
    a small human being
    again   . . .

I lie
beneath my blankets
    exhausted,
    exhilarated,
but slightly defeated

curled up
    fetus-like
    in a ball,
my eyelids are lined
with light

I giggle inside
    with joy

a child who,
    for a fraction of time,
has sneaked
into God's garden
and returned home
    safe
    again

a
moment
in time
is stolen
and devoured...

ONE MOMENT

a
language
of eyes
meets
across
a frozen room

a moment
in time
is stolen
and devoured

a long reverie
cast in seconds

then
the noise of life
    suspended
returns
and a lifetime
of maybes
is glimpsed
    and is gone

seen
　　through
　　　the eyes
　　　　of everything...

SOMETIMES

sometimes,

    a light like molten fire

    rushes through my veins,

    and a grin splits my face,

    so certain,

    that I must know everything

sometimes,

    there is nothing so fulfilling

    as the white tassel of a carpet

    seen through the eyes of everything,

    or a simple green pot

    sitting clean

    on a perfect surface

the
  reverie
    of
      a
        thousand
          lifetimes...

THE SUDDEN SCRAPING OF HEELS

the
sudden
sound
of my heel
scraping
on the floor
caused
my mind
to let go
of the reverie
of a thousand lifetimes

the
  glow
    of light
    that shines
  through
    morning
      trees
    and glints
  on early
dew...

THERE ARE ANGELS SNEAKING UP ON ME

there are angels
    sneaking up on me

I know,
    because
from the corner of my eye
I see bright flapping wings
    that are golden,
    then are gone

angels are sneaking up on me

    I never quite see them
    but they run giggling
    down the stairs ahead of me

I see them in the glow of light
that shines through morning trees
    and glints on early dew

there are angels sneaking up on me

I know,
    because
    I hear their laughter
    in my heart

galaxies
so
tender...

A HEART FULL OF GALAXIES

my
heart
is thick
and warm
and full of galaxies
so tender
they make
me
want
to
cry

as
   constant
      as
        the
        moon
        and
        honest
      as
     empty
space...

PLACES IN MY HEART

there are places
in my heart
    so sacred
    that no one can go there

so huge in their unspokeness
    that no voice dare sound

there are flowers in my heart
    whose petals,
    when unfolding,
touch me
    as gentle
    as a soft wind

there is a steady flame in my heart,
    unflickering,
as constant as the moon
    and honest
    as empty space

my
    body,
        light,
            floats
                into
                    space...

MY HANDS CRADLE THE MOON

I lie
on the floor
and galaxies swirl
above me

my hands cradle the moon
and juggle stars

my body,
light,
floats into space

I have no structure,
only form

thin and diaphanous
and able to live
forever

my father, the poet...

I began writing poetry later on in life; so did my father. After working in sales and insurance for forty years, he retired in 1986 at the age of sixty-one.

Finding himself with too much time on his hands, he signed up for writing classes at the University of the Third Age, a marvelous institution in Great Britain that offers free classes to senior citizens. At first, he wanted to take the writing class only if no poetry was involved. Two years later, at the urging of his writing teacher, he began poetry classes.   • • •

He writes mainly about the Welsh and Yorkshire landscape that he loves so much, and his poems reveal a creative and sensitive side to his nature that I never had the chance to experience when I was young. Dad now helps teach poetry classes himself. Recently we had a long transatlantic phone conversation about the merits of free verse, something I could never have imagined taking place before.

These two poems were written shortly after he began his first poetry class.

THE TURNING POINT

slowly we left the valley of Betws-y-Coed,
all greens, bright and somber

soaring trees of magnificent splendor,
gently climbing, rain-cleansed

ever hopeful of better things,
we arrived at Cape Curig,
the turning point

Capel Curig: lonely but not lonely,
cold and castaway,
but home to weary limbs—
end of the road to some,
beginning of the road for us

• • •

turning the corner to another world,
an all-encompassing windscreen vista
of breathtaking, rain-swept mountains,
starkly gleaming in the pouring rain—
a thousand flashes of whitened torrents
spilling down the mountainside

going where?

this land of running water,
the thundering music of the mountains—
Pier Gynt personified
in a Welsh landscape of supreme beauty

clouds billowed,
revealing a snow-capped peak:
snowed on Snowdon

gleams of ice-rimmed rocks,

. . .

black on brown, white on gray
gray on brown, black on white—
an ever-changing world of color and sense

a lake intruded—
black water of styx-like memory

metamorphic rocks straddled the mountainside;
historic beauty
that conjured up deep Celtic feelings
of past sedimentary changes.

eagles soared in glorious freedom,
though savage at the end—
a payment for this hurting beauty

another day, another passing

—*bob ellis*

the
    lullaby
        of
            running
                water
                    permeated
                        the
                            quiet...

THE LULLABY OF RUNNING WATER

the fog hung heavy on the escarpment—
wet, dank and indecipherable in its grayness

lower down the winding, narrow road
the fog retreated to a cloudy clear day

the car splashed through running water
between crumbling dry stone walls
thick with dirty green mossiness

miniature waterfalls crossed the road,
gurgling merrily down the hill

leaving the car in the valley bottom,
the silence struck

curlews cried

the lullaby of running water
permeated the quiet

· · ·

the beck was full of peat-colored water
rushing down the stone-lined channel;
foam hugged the corners

eddies of detritus clung to the bank—
a visible, risible chuckle of life-giving liquidity

climbing the steep bank,
squelching upwards in mud-slicked boots;
panting, struggling—
heavy jacket, heavier by the minute

all for the view—view indeed!

the vast water lay quiet
black
deep

. . .

unemotionally flat without ripples

beautifully indifferent
waiting, waiting,
for a cat's paw of wind-induced wavelettes

the eternal mystery of life encompassed
in one inspiring view

—*bob ellis*

A NEW BEGINNING

the tulips
of another day
may be the roses of
tomorrow....

thanks

Grateful thanks are due to all those who helped with this book.

To my parents who gave me life, and to Maharishi who gave it meaning; to my dear wife, Marion, for her love and friendship; to Rodney at 1st World Library who made it all possible, and to Michael for his beautiful cover design; to Martha, Shawna and Sali for their help editing; to Lynn and Brianna for their enthusiasm, and to Paul M. for his wise comments; and to Bindi, my friend.

To you and many others more—thank you.

about the authors

Tony Ellis was born in 1951 in Huddersfield, Yorkshire, an industrial city nestled in the Pennine Hills of northern England and once famous for its high quality woolen cloth. After graduating with an Honors Degree in Fine Art from the West of England College of Art in 1976, he devoted himself full-time to the study of meditation, and has been a teacher of Transcendental Meditation since 1977. This work led him to many parts of the world, including India, The Philippines, Switzerland and Holland. He now resides in Fairfield, Iowa, and Vancouver, B.C., with his wife, Marion, and apart from poetry, writes and produces books and films about spiritual life. He is currently at work on a second book of poetry entitled *The Morning Tree*.

. . .

His father, **Bob Ellis**, still lives in Huddersfield with his wife, Mary, and close to his daughter Pauline, his two granddaughters and three great-grandsons. He remains ever hopeful that one day Huddersfield Town, AFC, will be re-elected to the premier division of the English Football League.

For more information or to contact the author, visit www.tonyellis.com

A portion of the proceeds from this book go towards creating world peace.

www.ingramcontent.com/pod-product-compliance
Lightning Source LLC
Chambersburg PA
CBHW031851090426
42741CB00005B/438